M000164766

How to Tame the Tumbles

How to Tame the Tumbles
The Mindful Self-Compassionate Way

By
Eileen Beltzner

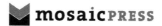

Library and Archives Canada Cataloguing in Publication

Title: How to tame the tumbles : the mindful self-compassionate way / by Eileen Beltzner.

Names: Beltzner, Eileen, 1950- author.

Identifiers: Canadiana (print) 2019009821X | Canadiana (ebook) 20190098287 | ISBN 9781771613866 (softcover) | ISBN 9781771613873 (HTML) | ISBN 9781771613880 (PDF) | ISBN 9781771613897 (Kindle)

Subjects: LCSH: Mindfulness (Psychology) | LCSH: Emotions in children. | LCSH: Compassion. | LCSH: Self.

Classification: LCC BF637.M56 B45 2019 | DDC 158.1/3—dc23

No part of this book may be reproduced or transmitted in any form, by any means, electronic or mechanical, including photocopying and recording, information storage and retrieval systems, without permission in writing from the publisher, except by a reviewer who may quote a brief passage in a review.

Published by Mosaic Press, Oakville, Ontario, Canada, 2019.

MOSAIC PRESS, Publishers
Copyright © Eileen Beltzner, 2019

ONTARIO ARTS COUNCIL
CONSEIL DES ARTS DE L'ONTARIO
an Ontario government agency
un organisme du gouvernement de l'Ontario

We acknowledge the Ontario Arts Council
for their support of our publishing program

Funded by the Government of Canada
Financé par le gouvernement du Canada

MOSAIC PRESS
1252 Speers Road, Units 1 & 2
Oakville, Ontario L6L 5N9
phone: (905) 825-2130
info@mosaic-press.com

For Parents and Children

Praise for this Book

"*How to Tame the Tumbles the Mindful Self-Compassionate Way,* is a funny, engaging story that teaches children how to be kinder and more supportive to themselves when experiencing difficult emotions. There are very few books written for kids on self-compassion, and this one is sure to be a classic. Parents who read this wonderful story with their children can help them learn one of the most important lessons in life: It's not what happens to you, but how you treat yourself when times are tough - as an inner friend or an inner enemy - that determines our ability to succeed and thrive."

- Kristin Neff, Ph.D.
Associate Professor, The University of Texas at Austin, and author of *The Mindful Self-Compassion Workbook & Self-Compassion: The Proven Power of Being Kind to Yourself &* Co-author of *The Mindful Self-Compassion Workbook*

"*How to Tame the Tumbles the Mindful Self-Compassionate Way,* offers simple powerful practices to support children and adults in, as I like to say, having our feelings without our feelings having us and making us say and do things we regret."

- Dr. Amy Saltzman
Director of the Association for Mindfulness in Education, and author of *A Still Quiet Place*

"As an educator and a grandmother, I am so excited to see this book come to print. Eileen has used this vehicle to transport both children and parents through very difficult terrain, emotional regulation. Offering bite size pieces of understanding and then actual practices that will help parents (or teachers) talk about and practice what to do when the inevitable difficult emotions must be navigated. I especially appreciate the non-judgmental elements embedded throughout this wonderful educational children's book."

- Patricia Ward, M.Ed. Educational Consultant & Mindful Schools Guiding Teacher

"*How to Tame the Tumbles the Mindful Self-Compassionate Way* is a fun, interactive resource for children and people who care about them. It introduces language and practices which can help children to cultivate awareness of their emotions, and to begin to respond to whatever is arising in a healthier way. In so doing, it provides parents and teachers with the capacity to teach children skills, which they themselves may never have been taught.

- Dr. Alison Kelford, MHSc, CCFP, FCFP

"With her years of experience in the mental health field, Eileen writes with gentle wisdom and quiet humour a story about Isabella Esmeralda, a child struggling with self-regulation and anger management along with the hurt of lost friendships which are the result. Teachers, parents, indeed anyone who works with children will recognize the need for and will welcome with relief this wonderful book. It is fun to read with a child and the step-by-step instructions to learn self and anger management are easy to follow. Put simply, this is an outstanding resource."

- Mary Walker, BA, Honours Psych, Cert. Ed.

"Few lessons in life are more important than learning to tame our "tumbles" and Eileen Beltzner has found a delightful, informative and fun way to support kids and their parents to contend with the inevitable hard emotions that everyone faces. This book is a brilliant and eminently helpful application of the groundbreaking self-compassion work of Drs. Kristin Neff and Chris Germer, brought to life through the eyes of Isabella Esmeralda Anastasia Pookapoo and the whole Pookapoo family. Read this book. Read it again with your child who has a case of the tumbles. And together you will find a delightful way to tame them."

- Steven D. Hickman, Psy.D.
Clinical Psychologist,
Founding Director, UCSD Center for Mindfulness

Table of Contents

Foreword

Haven't we all experienced the tumbles—those regretful moments when a bushel of angry words tumble out of our mouths and we can't take them back? We might spend awhile justifying ourselves, but let's face it; we wish it just never happened. The cost to our peace of mind and our relationships is just too high. When parents assess the cost in their own lives, they are usually determined to find a way to protect their children from the same fate. But how?

Emotion regulation is a hot topic these days. One of the underlying factors in emotion regulation is self-compassion, or inner compassion. Just reflect for a minute, as Eileen Beltzner invites us to do in this book, how we feel when a loving person listens to us and comforts us when things go wrong in our lives. Self-compassion is the skill of doing that for ourselves, when we need it the most, and it can have a profound effect on our lives.

Burgeoning research on self-compassion demonstrates that self-compassion is associated with a wide range of positive psychological factors including enhanced achievement, motivation, a sense of wellbeing, emotional resilience, reduced stress, anxiety and depression, a stronger immune system, healthy life habits such as diet and exercise, and wisdom. Self-compassion also provides a foundation for relating compassionately with others and thereby improves our relationships.

At our mindful self-compassion trainings for adults, someone inevitably asks, "How do we teach this to kids? I could have been spared so much difficulty in life if only someone taught me about self-compassion when I was young!" My impression is that kids actually learn self-compassion more easily than adults because they have not had the many years of cultural conditioning, especially striving for perfection and harshly criticizing themselves when things go wrong. Most young children still believe that they are worthy of kindness when they suffer, fail, or feel inadequate. We just need to teach them how to give it to themselves.

Eileen Beltzner's charming book gets right to the heart of the matter in a disarming way. Rather than teaching these important skills directly, in a manner that kids would be inclined to resist, she forms a narrative and deftly engages parents in the teaching aspect without departing from the story. As a reader, I can easily imagine the joy of engaging in this process with kids and watching them internalize these skills while their hearts and minds are still relatively innocent and open. I also think I would be reminded to practice self-compassion myself in a simpler, more childlike manner—just the way it ought to be practiced.

As our world becomes increasingly fast-paced and our interactions with others are mediated by technology like the internet, I think it is becoming increasingly important for parents to deliberately teach inner skills that children can use to slow down their minds and focus on the present moment, and also to help kids deal with difficult emotions like loneliness and anger that are likely to proliferate in coming years. Eileen Beltzner, who has worked with kids and adults for the past 40 years as a social worker and a clinician, has her finger on the pulse and has also found a delightful way to make her insights come alive for children and their parents. I hope this book tumbles into the hands of many people for years to come.

Christopher Germer, PhD
Lecturer on Psychiatry, Harvard Medical School
Author, *The Mindful Path to Self-Compassion*
& Co-author of The Mindful Self-Compassion
Workbook: A Proven Way to Accept Yourself, Build Inner
Strength, and Thrive

Preface

As parents, many of us have spent a lot of time and energy making sure our children brush their teeth on a daily basis. However, how many parents devote as much time helping their children deal with their anger in a way that doesn't hurt them or others? Many parents don't even know how to do this. In fact, some parents often have great difficulty managing their own anger.

Anger is a healthy emotion that many people sometimes have a problem expressing in a healthy and non-harming way. It can cause a lot of hurt when it spirals out of control, causing us problems and overshadowing our *best self*.

As a child growing up and later as a Registered Social Worker and a Child and Family Therapist, I've seen up close and personal the negative results of anger that had spiraled out of control; and the hurt it caused to the people it was directed towards and also to those who had witnessed it.

It is my hope that the MSC concepts and practices that are woven throughout this book will allow both the parent's and the child's *best self* to show up most often. My intent is to help parents and children go a long way in undoing the many negative psychological effects a person may have developed because anger was their boss instead of the other way around.

This book teaches simple, concrete, hands on practices to help *be* with anger...*better*. To quote the late Maya Angelo, a civil rights activist and poet, "I did then what I knew how to do. Now that I know better, I do better."

Over the years, my work has always aimed at improving the lives of children through the adults who love and care for them. My wish is parents will have some fun reading this book together with their child and both will learn some emotional regulation skills that are researched based and backed by some of the most recent discoveries in neuroscience.

How to Use This Book

This book is for children between the ages of 7 to 12 years of age and meant to be a learning experience for both child and parent. I suggest the parent read the book first; by doing this you will become familiar with both MSC *adult-sized* and MSC *child-sized* concepts and practices in the book.

For the emotional resiliency skills taught in this book to become second nature to both of you, I suggest taking turns guiding each other through the various practices. In the beginning, do this when difficult moments are *not* present and only if your child is willing. Most children will enjoy a two-way learning experience. It might even be fun!

Who Else Might Find This Book Helpful?

This book is also for professionals. I have been told by a number of elementary and resource teachers that this book has a place in every elementary classroom. Other professionals such as Social Workers, Family Physicians, Child and Family Therapists, Psychologists, Child Psychiatrists, Pediatricians and Child Care Workers will, no doubt, recognize the MSC concepts and practices in this book as useful tools that will assist them in their therapeutic work with children and families.

Notes and Resources

The reader will find at the end of this book, a notes and resource section, with extra content, instructional videos and audio files. I hope by giving the reader and listener this additional information their understanding of why certain elements are contained in *How to Tame the Tumbles the Mindful Self-Compassionate Way* will be deepened. Also, if the reader or listener wishes to connect to up-to-date resources in the fields of Mindfulness and Mindful Self-Compassion, this section will make that possible.

Chapter 1

Only One Friend Left

There was a little girl whose name was Isabella Esmeralda Anastasia Pookapoo. She lived with her Mommy and Papa not too far from where you live. The only friend she had left shared her bed with her every night. His name was Pookie and he was the family dog.

Why was her dog the only friend she had left? There were three reasons. The first reason was Isabella didn't like anyone telling her what to do. The second reason was she wanted to be the best at everything she tried. And, the third reason was Isabella wanted to be the boss of everyone and everything. I'm sure you know that's just not the way the world works. Big trouble was headed her way. Soon Isabella would find out exactly what that big trouble was.

What Isabella wanted was not what she got and she spent a lot of her time feeling mad. When the sun was too hot, she got mad. When it rained, she got mad. When her sandwich wasn't made the way she liked it, she got mad. And when she wasn't allowed to stay up as late as *she* wanted to...guess what? Isabella got mad.

1

When Isabella got mad at home, she would cry and scream and holler and stomp her feet. And then, mean, hurtful and unkind words would start *falling* right out of her mouth. I'm not going to tell you the words she said. I am sure you can guess what some of them might be.

"Her friends at school liked Isabella because sometimes she could be quite funny. Sometimes she could even be kind."

But when Isabella started to behave the same way with her friends as she did with her parents, especially if she didn't like the games they wanted to play, or if one of them could skip faster than she could, big trouble finally caught up with her.

One day at recess, while playing tag, a friend tagged her. Isabella refused to be *it*. She said if this friend didn't go tag someone else right away, she would tell everyone this girl's breath smelled like a dog's fart and she still wore diapers to bed!

Of course, the girl started crying. And when all the kids came over to find out what was wrong, she was brave. She told them exactly what Isabella had said to her.

Well, that was it! No one wanted to play with Isabella after that. So now you know why she only had one friend.

"The only reason her dog was still her friend was because he had a kind heart."

Pookie knew Isabella was unhappy. Sometimes at night, he could hear her crying. He sure hoped her parents could find a way to help her.

Chapter 2

What's a Tumble Problem?

Isabella jumped down from the school bus and ran into her apartment building. She ran up two flights of stairs. She was crying. When she unlocked the front door, she was so glad to see her Mommy and Papa were home from work. Isabella ran over to them. They could easily see she was crying. Her tears were so big they rolled down the middle of her cheeks and wet the underside of her chin.

"What are the tears about Isabella?" Mommy asked.

"What's wrong?" Papa asked.

"I'll tell you what's wrong. Nobody wants to play with me, that's what's wrong! All my friends hate me."

"How do you know that Isabella?" Papa asked.

"Well, do your friends make faces at you Papa? Do they laugh and point at you? Do they say, "here comes Meanie Poo – run for your lives" when they see you coming? Well, do they Papa?"

"Well, no, they don't," he answered.

"Well mine do," Isabella shouted. And with that, she fell down to the floor and cried and cried and cried.

Her Mommy sat down on the floor and hugged her. Next Papa sat down on the floor and hugged her. It took a long time for her sobs to turn into sniffles but when they did, her Mommy gave Isabella a few tissues to blow her stuffed up nose.

With *knowing look faces,* both parents nodded their heads up and down. Mr. Pookapoo had often behaved exactly like Isabella did when he was a kid, and he did so even when he was much older. Fortunately for him, he developed a plan that helped him to be more of the funny, kind person he really was.

Because of his experience Papa knew Isabella would have to work hard at learning ways to be with her *big feelings of anger and upset* when the world wasn't the way she wanted it to be. Now was the time. She had no friends left to play with and she wanted some. She was also the right age to participate in the plan.

Her Mommy and Papa sat silently for a few minutes. Isabella wondered what would happen next. Her Papa was the first to break the silence. "We have known for a long time that you have a tumble problem," he said.

"Isabella scrunched up her tear-stained face and scratched her head, "What's a tumble problem?"

"Okay," said her Papa, "let me explain it to you this way.

"The word tumble, means to fall. When you get mad Isabella mean, hurtful and unkind words fall out of your mouth."

That's true thought Isabella. That does happen.

4

"And, now your friends have had enough. They don't want to play with you and now they're being mean to you."

"You are in a tough situation Isabella that needs to be figured out.

"A tough situation that needs to be figured out is called a problem. So, when you put the two words together, tumble and problem, you get tumble problem."

Pookie had been pretending he was fast asleep on the couch as all this crying, hugging and talking was going on. He quite liked what Mr. Pookapoo had said. Pookie also thought Mr. Pookapoo had explained it very well.

Now Isabella's Mommy took a turn talking. "It's not so much that you get mad Isabella. Everybody gets mad sometimes. It's that you say mean things to people when you do. That is *never* okay. I think that's why kids are calling you a Meanie Poo. You often act like one!"

Of course Isabella started crying again. She was remembering how embarrassed she had felt when all the kids had laughed at her. Most of all, she was crying because she liked having friends and now she didn't have any. She felt hopeless inside.

Pookie stopped pretending he was fast asleep. He stood up on his paws, gave himself a shake and ran over to Isabella. He nuzzled his little black nose into the crook of her neck; then began licking the tears off her face. Pookie was trying desperately to comfort Isabella; and, to let her know that just because she thought she didn't have any friends left; it wasn't true. He was still her friend.

"Thoughts are not always facts."

"Pookie also knew hopeless feelings don't last forever. Feelings like that can often change quickly...just like the weather. "

Chapter 3

Surprised Big Time

Pookie was so right. Isabella didn't have to feel hopeless for long. What her Papa said next almost *knocked her socks right off.* Isabella was surprised big time!

"When I was a kid Isabella, no one wanted to play with me either. I had a bad case of the tumbles, even worse than you have. I know it'll get better for you; it did for me."

"You had a tumble problem too?"

"I sure did," her Papa answered.

"Even worse than me?"

"Absolutely," he said. "And, I'll tell you something else Isabella.

"There are over 7 billion people in the world. Thousands and thousands of them, kids and grown-ups too, have tumble problems."

So you see, there are thousands of people who often act like *Meanie Poos* too."

"Wow!" exclaimed Isabella. "That's a lot of people who may not have any friends to play with."

"That's *true*," said her Mommy. "So you see Isabella, you're not alone. And, if your Papa hadn't learned ways to have less tumbles, ... he'd still be one of those grown-ups who often acts like a *Meanie Poo* today."

"How come your parents didn't help you when you were a kid Papa?" asked Isabella.

"They tried their best. They read books and asked lots of experts what to do. They were told that time-out was the answer to my problem. So that's what they did."

"What's time-out Papa?" asked Isabella.

"Let me explain it to you this way. When I had the tumbles, my parents would tell me to go to my room. I wouldn't do it. I'd be carried to my room, kicking and screaming. I would scream and cry and even throw things around in there. When I was finally quiet, my parents would tell me I could come out. That's *time-out*."

"Did it help to stop the tumbles?" asked Isabella.

"No." said her Papa.

"What did you learn?" asked Isabella.

"I learned how to be *quiet* so I could get *out* of my room!"

Isabella's tearful face wasn't looking quite as sad anymore. She looked up at her Papa and said, "I think I have a tumble problem too, just like you had Papa."

"Would you like us to help you with that?" her Papa asked.

Isabella nodded her head up and down and smiled.

Pookie had been sitting quietly nearby and listening to every word felt a smile forming inside his heart. Pookie knew what her parents had just said to Isabella would help her feel a lot better inside. Now Isabella knew two things she didn't know before. One, she wasn't the only one who had a tumble problem and often acted like a

Meanie Poo and two, there was hope she might get her friends back.

"How did you stop getting mad Papa?" asked Isabella.

"Oh…I've never stopped getting mad. I've just mostly stopped having the tumbles when I get mad. I have learned how to *be* with my mad feelings, without my mad feelings *being the boss of me.*"

That way, I have a better chance of not saying mean things I'll regret later," her Papa answered. "And tomorrow is a good day for us to start practicing. It's Saturday and we'll all be home."

"Begin practicing for what?" asked Isabella.

"Begin practicing ways to tame the tumbles of course," answered her Mommy. "But that's enough talking for now. Let's have a snack."

Pookie's short, stubby white tail started wagging furiously. He was delighted to hear Mrs. Pookapoo say snack; it meant he would be getting something to eat. He was happy about that. His tummy had been making empty rumbling sounds for quite awhile.

Chapter 4

Go Slow to Go Fast

Today was Saturday and was the day Isabella was to begin learning ways that might help get her friends back. She jumped out of bed quickly and almost knocked Pookie to the floor. She ran straight into her parent's bedroom. Unfortunately, it was only 5:00 AM and her parents were fast asleep. She ordered them to wake up. Her Mommy opened one eye and told her to go back into her bedroom and color or read or something, until their alarm clock rang at 6:30.

As she waited for the alarm to go off, she was growing more and more impatient. It was taking such a long time. Finally she couldn't stand it anymore. She threw her crayons on her bedroom floor, ran right into their bedroom and in a booming voice shouted, "GET OUT OF BED NOW. I WANT MY FRIENDS BACK FAST!"

Of course, her parents were now wide-awake. Isabella's voice was loud enough to wake up each and every sleeping polar bear in the Arctic Circle. However, her parents continued to stay in their bed. They were never going to allow Isabella to boss them around, no matter how loudly she screamed.

When her parents finally came out of their bedroom, her Mommy sat down beside her and quietly said, "Isabella, we don't like being shouted at. We are happy you want to learn about ways to tame the tumbles but it won't be fast. If you go too fast in the beginning when you are learning something new, you can make a lot of mistakes. And if that happens, you'll have to spend more time learning how to do it.

"Sometimes you need to go slow to go fast, Isabella."

We are going to eat breakfast and you will have to wait."

"But both of you are so slow when you eat breakfast," whined Isabella.

Her Papa took in a deep breath and let it out slowly. "Tumble taming is hard work Isabella and I need to eat. If I don't eat I get grouchy."

After they finished breakfast her parents asked Isabella if she had any questions about what they had talked about the night before.

"Yes, I do. What does the word *tame* mean?" she asked.

"Let me explain it to you this way," answered her Papa. "Do you remember when Pookie was a puppy and he would nip and scratch us when he hadn't seen us for awhile? He was so excited to see us."

"Yes, I do," said Isabella. "Sometimes his scratches really hurt."

"Well, your Mommy and I taught him ways to be with his excitement that didn't hurt people,

that's what tame means. Does that help you understand?" asked her Papa.**"**

With a puzzled look on her face, Isabella answered, "I think so."

She kind of understood how her Papa had explained it but not really. She wasn't a puppy and she didn't nip and scratch people. At least not yet!

Chapter 5

More Talking, More Listening...UGH

"So, let's explain a few things to you before we begin the practices," said her Mommy.

Isabella wanted action not more talking. But she would have to wait. Luckily, she was sitting on the couch in the living room with Pookie curled up on her lap. Somehow his warm body and the sound of his breathing helped with the waiting. Her parents sat across from her on separate chairs.

"Isabella," asked her Papa, "have you learned anything at school about what to do if there is a fire?"

"Yes," Isabella answered proudly. "Keep calm is what my teacher says. And we practice fire drills so we know where the exits are. And, if I catch on fire, I'm to stop, drop and roll."

"There are also ways to prevent many fires from even getting started," her Mommy added, "like never play with matches, or always blow out a lit candle before you leave a room."

Pookie knew what he would do if there was a fire – he would bark, but what about the tumble taming? He wished her parents would get to the point. Finally, Mrs. Pookapoo did.

"Just as there are ways to prevent fires from getting started Isabella, there are ways to prevent many of our tumbles from even getting started. And we practice these ways almost everyday."

"You do?" Isabella asked.

"Yes, we do. And, we have some ideas on how we can teach these ways to you."

"What kind of ways Mommy?" Isabella asked.

"Oh, we'll be doing some *elevator riding* practices. And, I almost forgot ... a carpentry lesson too."

"Whew! This sounds like it could be fun," thought Isabella.

"So, here's what you need to know when it comes to tumble taming," said Papa. "In the beginning, tumbles that have already started are much like a fire that is out of control. It's too late to prevent the fire or for us to put it out. We need to call the fire department for help. It's the fire fighters job to put the fire out."

Isabella's *fun face* turned suddenly into *a worried looking face*. "But, what happens to me if my tumbles have already started?" she asked.

"Who ever is home at the time will stay close to you when that happens," her Papa answered.

"You never did that before," said Isabella.

"We've thought about this Isabella and we have decided you need one of us with you," he answered. "When either Mommy or I *almost* get the tumbles, it feels like a small fire has started to burn inside us and it feels awful."

"You actually get the tumbles Isabella," said her Mommy.

14

"And when you get the tumbles, it must feel like you have a full blown forest fire raging inside you.**"**

Her Mommy stopped talking for a moment... then in a comforting and soothing kind of voice she said,

"If that's so Isabella, it must feel really scary inside you."Now Isabella was paying attention to what her Mommy was saying. Her parents really did understand!**"**

"But how can staying with me help?" asked Isabella.

"We're there beside you, to lend you our calm, until the forest fire burns out or is put out," answered her Papa.**"**

"And, it'll be your job to let us know when you notice that has happened."

"How can I let you know that?" Isabella asked.

"How would you like to let us know?" asked her Papa.

"I could touch your hand or arm or something like that."

"Sounds good to me," said her Mommy.

"Sounds good to me," said her Papa.

"So you and Papa will be like firefighters," Isabella asked.

"And you'll stay with me until I notice the fire is out?"

"You've got it!" he said.

"We don't have sirens, fire engines or long hoses," Mommy added with a grin. "We just have love."

"But how will I notice the fire is out?"

"We hope the tumble taming plan will help you with that," said her Mommy.

"You'll just have to wait and see," said her Papa.

Pookie barked twice, as if to say, "This is really starting to get interesting."

Chapter 6

You Can't Get It Wrong

Mommy stood up from her chair. She stretched and yawned. "I think we've all had enough talking for now," she said. "Let's have a snack first and start practicing after that."

Pookie ears perked up, his head cocked to one side and he licked his lips. He loved being part of this family; they were always hungry, just like him.

After the snack of apple pieces, graham crackers and cheese cubes, Isabella flopped down on the couch beside her Papa. He looked at her with a big smile on his face and said, "Now, I'm going to teach you about breathing."

Isabella also smiled and started to giggle, "Papa, I know how to breathe," she said.

"Not this way," he said. "This is a special way of breathing; *a noticing stuff way.*"

"A noticing stuff way!" exclaimed Isabella. "What the heck is that?" she asked.

"Instead of telling you what it is," answered her Papa, "I'll show you. Please watch carefully."

"When I start to feel mad showing up inside me," he said, "This is what I do. I take in one breath of air through my nose and out of my nose it comes, ... and then another in and another out, ...in and out, ...over and over again." Then he was quiet and just sat there on the couch breathing.

Isabella was quiet too. She wanted to watch carefully to figure out what was so special about her Papa's breathing. After trying her best to see, she decided there wasn't anything special. He was breathing – just like he breathed every day. And all this watching was really getting boring. To entertain herself, Isabella placed herself in such a way that she could stare right up her Papa's nose. What she saw there started her giggling again - much, much louder than she had before. Her Papa had the hairiest nostrils she had ever seen in her whole life! And she told him so.

Mommy laughed. Papa didn't. He looked at her with his *serious parent face* and said, "As best as you can Isabella, please pay attention. This is important."

"But I was paying attention!" exclaimed Isabella. "What did I miss seeing?"

"You were breathing like you always do Papa. I didn't see anything special about your breathing."

"That's because what was special about my breathing was going on inside my brain. There is no way you could have seen that Isabella, even if you had been staring up my nose the whole time."

As he continued talking, Isabella could tell he was holding back a smile.

"My brain, actually my mind, was *noticing stuff* that I had decided I wanted to pay attention to," he said. "That's what made it a special kind of breathing."

"What kind of stuff were you noticing Papa?"

"I was noticing where I could feel the air the most as I breathed in and as I breathed out. Today, I felt it at the tip of my nose. Sometimes, I decide to pay attention to the sound or the rhythm of my breathing."

"Do you notice any other stuff Mommy?" Isabella asked.

"Sometimes I do. I might decide to notice if the air feels cool or warm in my nose or at the back of my throat as I breathe. Other times, I'll just notice if my tummy is moving in and out."

"How can you remember all that?" Isabella asked.

"We practice," answered both her parents, at exactly the same time.

Isabella's *discouraged looking face* was easy for her parents to spot.

"What's wrong?" asked her Mommy.

"I won't be able to do it. I'll do something wrong."

Her Mommy placed her hand tenderly on Isabella's cheek and in a soothing and comforting kind of voice said,

"Awwwww, my little sweetheart, you can't get it wrong. It's simply paying attention to what you have been doing since you were born... breathing."

The only thing that's different is choosing to notice something while you are breathing ... and then coming back to it over and over again."

"And the only way to learn how it's done is to practice noticing over and over again," said her Papa.

So that's exactly what they practiced together on and off all that day.

Later that evening, after dinner and after Isabella had washed her face and hands, brushed her teeth, put on her PJ's and climbed into bed; Isabella's Mommy reminded her of something that helped Isabella be less worried about getting it wrong.

"When you learned how to ride your bicycle, no one talked about getting it right or wrong. You just practiced and after awhile you could do it."

Learning ways to help tame most of your tumbles will be just the same."

"I love you so much Mommy," Isabella said. Her Mommy tenderly touched Isabella on her cheek and said, "I love you more, my Isabella Esmeralda Anastasia Pookapoo." After kissing Isabella on her forehead, she left the bedroom.

Not long after, Pookie, who was cuddled up next to Isabella on her bed - took in one big breath of air and then let it out. "Ahhhhhhhh," he sighed. It was not any old sigh. It was a big sigh of relief. Pookie could finally stop worrying about his little human friend Isabella. Her Mommy and Papa knew what to do.

Chapter 7

Elevator Riding

The next morning was Sunday. It was another whole day Pookie got to spend with his family. Grown-up Pookapoos did not go off to work and Isabella had no school to attend.

Isabella had already been awake for a long time. Pookie was worried if Isabella was sick or something. She wasn't behaving or sounding like her *normal* self. Isabella hadn't raced into her parent's bedroom as soon as she woke up. She waited until their alarm clock rang. And, she did not scream at them to get up as she sometimes had. Instead, she asked her parents, in a much quieter voice than Pookie had ever heard her speak, "What's next?"

"A slow breakfast is next," answered her Mommy, "and some elevator riding after that."

"But we don't have an elevator in our building," Isabella said laughing.

"Of course we don't. We have three of them, right here inside this room!" exclaimed her Mommy.

Isabella's brown eyes opened wide. She looked at her Mommy and she looked at her Papa. He was nodding in agreement.

"Each of us has our own personal elevator inside our body," he said.

"Okay, if that's true," said Isabella, "why haven't my teachers ever mentioned it before?"

"We don't have a real elevator inside us Isabella," he answered. "We have something like an elevator inside us - our mind."

"And, just like elevators can move people inside a tall building from one floor to another, our minds can move our attention from one part of our body to another," said Mommy.

"And we hope elevator riding will help you to experience moving your attention, up and down inside your body, *on purpose,* too."

Pookie was looking at Isabella. She looked confused. He sure was.

After they had finished a *slow* breakfast, Mommy said, "So let's begin." So, they began.

"First, I need to explain how this works," said Mrs. Pookapoo. "I'm going to ask you to imagine your body from the bottom of your feet to the top of your head, as a tall, sturdy building. Your building will have six floors inside it. The bottom of your feet will be the first floor or the ground floor, knees, the second floor... your belly button, the third floor, your heart in your chest area, the fourth floor, your neck, the fifth floor, and last but not least, your head will be the sixth or top floor. Any questions?"

"No questions," answered Papa.

"No questions," answered Isabella.

"Oh, I almost forgot," said Mrs. Pookapoo, "each time I call out a floor, you're to press your nose; it's the elevator button. It moves you to the floor I have called out. So now, please stand up."

"Isn't it best to *elevator ride* in bare feet?" asked Mr. Pookapoo.

"It sure is. So, please take off your socks and slippers," Mrs. Pookapoo answered.

Isabella had no idea what was going to happen next. She decided not to ask. She would wait and see.

Pookie sat still, listening and watching all of this. What an imagination his family had. He was so happy to hear Mr. Pookapoo tell Isabella it wasn't a *real* elevator. Pookie had been in a real elevator before. Going up and down in elevators always gave him a dizzy feeling in his brain.

Chapter 8

Eyes Closed ... Let's Go

"So let's begin. Closing your eyes, breathing in and breathing out, breathing in and breathing out. Not too fast and not too slow. Whatever is right, just for you." And now, imagining your body, from the bottom of your feet, to the top of your head as a tall, sturdy building."

"Mrs. Pookapoo was quiet for a few minutes. Sometimes it takes time to imagine things."

"Starting on the first floor, the bottom floor, feeling your toes and heels pressing against the floor and as you do, silently thanking your feet for everything they do for you every day. (*Pause*). Breathing in and breathing out...it's time to say goodbye to the first floor."

"Pressing your nose, moving up slowly to the second floor, feeling your knees as you bend them up and down, and thanking your knees for everything they do for you everyday. (*Pause*). Breathing in and breathing out, it's time to say goodbye to the second floor."

"Pressing your nose, moving up slowly to the third floor. Putting your hands on your belly, feeling your belly moving in and moving out, ... as you breathe in and out, ... thanking your belly for everything it does for you every day. (*Pause*). Breathing in and breathing out, it's time to say goodbye to the third floor."

"Pressing your nose, moving slowly to the fourth floor. Placing both your hands on your skin, over your heart area, feeling the warmth of your hands on your chest, thanking your heart for everything it does for you everyday. (*Pause*). Breathing in and breathing out, it's time to say goodbye to the fourth floor."

"Pressing your nose, moving slowly to the fifth floor. If you can move your head from side to side, you're there, thanking your neck for everything it does for you everyday. (*Pause*). Breathing in and breathing out, it's time to say goodbye to the fifth floor."

"Pressing the elevator button, moving slowly to the sixth floor, the top floor. If you can *notice* your eyes are closed, you're there, thanking your eyes for everything they do for you everyday. (*Pause*). Breathing in and breathing out, it's time to say goodbye to the sixth floor."

"Now pressing your nose each time you want to move from your top floor to the next floor below it ... stopping on each floor, taking your time and thanking that part of your body again as you move down to the ground floor. The neck...the heart area...the belly...the knees...the feet." A much longer pause followed.

The silence was finally interrupted by Mrs. Pookapoo's voice. "Has your elevator car reached the ground floor yet Isabella?"

"Yes, Mommy," said Isabella. And just as suddenly, as she had realized that, she realized something else. She could not only feel her toes and the bottom of her feet pressing against the floor, she could feel them from *the inside* of her body too!

"And now we'll go elevator riding over and over again," said Mrs. Pookapoo. "We can each take turns calling out which floors to stop on and, what to say, to thank the part of our body we've stopped on, before we move to the next floor. Eyes closed...let's go."

By dinnertime, Isabella had become an expert on the elevator floors inside her body. She was even able to move from floor to floor without pressing her nose.

❝And her body liked all the appreciation Isabella had sent its way.❞

After dinner, her Papa explained how elevator riding might help Isabella have fewer tumbles.

❝Knowing how to move my attention around inside my body Isabella really helped me to have fewer tumbles," he said.❞

"How Papa?" she asked.

"It helped me to notice what was happening *inside* me," he answered.

"What's so good about that?" Isabella asked.

"I got good at noticing if *a small fire* was starting inside me. When I noticed that, I did my tumble taming practices. The small fire inside me often remained small. Sometimes the fire was even put out," Papa answered.

Chapter 9

Mommy's Good Wishes Practice

The next evening, while they were all practicing elevator riding and the *noticing stuff way* of breathing, Isabella, who hadn't closed her eyes yet, noticed that when her Mommy took a breath in, her belly got bigger. And when she let a breath out, her belly got smaller. Isabella told her Mommy what she had noticed. She asked her Mommy if she would teach her how to do that.

"Of course I will Isabella," said her Mommy. "We'll need one of your stuffed animals though to help out."

Isabella raced into her bedroom to get Snowy the owl. Her Nana and Opa had given Snowy to her as a gift long before Isabella was even born. Snowy had been beside her in her crib when she was a baby. Now, Snowy slept in Isabella's big girl bed every night.

Isabella returned with Snowy in hand.

"So lie down on your back Isabella," said her Mommy.

Isabella did just that.

"Now Isabella, please put Snowy on your belly. This is how to *belly button breathe*," said her Mommy. "First, take a big breath in and *see* what happens to Snowy."

Isabella took a big breath in and saw Snowy move up towards the ceiling.

"Next," said Mommy, "slowly let that breath out and see what happens to Snowy."

Isabella slowly let her breath out and saw Snowy move down towards the floor.

"Now Isabella we'll practice belly button breathing together."

And they did. Up and down...up and down...up and down went Snowy.

"You've got it, " said her Mommy.

"Belly button breathing is another practice that helps me keep a small fire starting inside me – small!"

Day after day, Isabella's parents practiced with her. Her Mommy was so right. The more Isabella practiced elevator riding and the noticing stuff way of breathing, the easier it was to remember everything. It was just like practicing to be able to ride her bicycle.

The same thing happened with belly button breathing too. Every night, just before Isabella went to sleep, she would put Snowy on her tummy. Up and down Snowy would go just as fast or as slow as Isabella decided Snowy's ride should be. After that, Isabella, Pookie and Snowy would snuggle up together and drift off to sleep.

One evening, before her Mommy kissed her goodnight, Isabella asked, "Are there practices you do Mommy that you haven't taught me?"

"There is one," her Mommy answered. "I call it my *good wishes practice*."

"What's that Mommy?"

"Well, every night before I fall asleep, I send you wishes for happiness, for health and strength, for safety and for kindness."

"I like those wishes Mommy. Could I wish those wishes for me too?" she asked.

"Of course you can!"

"How?" Isabella asked.

"Just say; … "May I be happy."… "May I be healthy and strong." … "May I be safe."… "May I be kind to myself and to others.**"**

It's that easy. I'll practice the wishes with you if you like Isabella, so you'll remember them."

"Okay Mommy. I'd like that. Is it okay for me to say those words for Pookie?" Isabella asked.

With a big smile on her face, her Mommy answered.

"You can say those wishes for every living being on the planet earth.**"**

"That's a lot of wishes to say," Isabella said laughing.

"Yes, it is Isabella. Let's just start with you and Pookie tonight. Otherwise both of us will be awake all night saying wishes."

And that is just what Isabella and her Mommy did.

Pookie loved all the *good wishes* they sent his way. And he sent them right back to Isabella, her Mommy, and her Papa.

The next day while Isabella was getting ready for school, her Mommy told her something else about the good wishes practice. "Sometimes, when I am at work and I am having a hard day, I do the good wishes practice too," she said.

"Why would you have a hard day?" Isabella asked. She couldn't believe that grown-ups had hard days like she had at school.

"Do you remember when we told you that sometimes there are grown-ups that often act like *Meanie Poos*?" her Mommy asked.

"Yes, I remember," said Isabella.

"Well, there are a few of those grown-ups at my work. Sometimes, when they behave that way towards me, I say the good wishes practice."

"For the *Meanie Poos* at your work?" Isabella asked.

Her Mommy smiled, "First Isabella, I say the good wishes for myself, so I don't get the tumbles and behave like a *Meanie Poo* too!"

"But of course," said her Mommy, "After I've said the good wishes for me a few times, I say them for the grown-ups who are behaving like *Meanie Poos* that day."

"Really?" asked Isabella.

"Really!" exclaimed Mommy.

"Wow!" said Isabella.

"Double wow!" said her Mommy.

Chapter 10

Papa's Comforting Friend Practice

When Papa came home from work that night, Isabella told him that her Mommy had taught her the *good wishes practice*. "Are there practices you do Papa, that you didn't tell me about yet?" she asked.

"There is one," he answered. But, before I explain it to you, I want you to know something important about mad feelings."

"Okay," Isabella said.

"I've learned that *mad* can be tricky. A small fire could be inside me without me even knowing it's there. It would get bigger and bigger and suddenly – a tumble would *fly* right out of my mouth."

"Oh, oh...that's not so good Papa."

"But, I learned a way to outsmart mad," he said, "so that doesn't happen very often any more."

"What kind of way?" Isabella asked.

"I have learned that even before I know I'm getting mad, my body knows. I know what my body feels like inside when mad is starting."

"How do you know?" asked Isabella.

"From some of the ways my body *reacts* that show me mad is coming. When I notice that, I do *my comforting friend practice.*"

"How do you do that?" asked Isabella.

"You already do it with Pookie," Papa answered, "when there is a big, loud thunder storm outside."

"I do?"

"Yes, you do Isabella. When Pookie gets frightened in a thunder storm and his little body shakes, what do you do?"

"I hold him close. I say *there, there* to him in a soft voice. I tell him he's safe and I give him a big, long hug."

"And what happens when you do all that Isabella?"

"He stops shaking so much. He licks my face. He's not so afraid anymore."

"So you soothe and comfort him?"

"Yes, I guess I do," Isabella answered.

"Well, when I start to notice certain reactions in my body ... maybe say I'm pressing my teeth together or my chest feels tight, I know mad is starting up. So, I soothe and comfort myself... just like you do for Pookie when he feels afraid."

"How do you do that by *yourself* Papa?"

"First I take a few breaths in and out. And after that...I say, hmmm, *mad* is here. Ouch! This hurts. Next, I remind myself millions of people sometimes feel *mad* too. I'm not alone. After that, I put my hand on my heart or the back of my neck, like Mommy puts her hand on your cheek when you are upset...and I say words to myself in my head, that I really need to hear right in that moment. And I say the words in a soft, kind and caring voice."

"What kind of words Papa?" Isabella asked.

"Words maybe like…May I remember how hard I try; or, May I be strong; or May I be patient. Sometimes I even say May I accept myself as I am.**"**

"And after that Papa?" Isabella asked.

"For some reason, usually my chest isn't tight anymore. I'm not clenching my jaw. It's like I have *a good friend inside me,* and that friend comforted me."

Isabella smiled and said, "Just like you and Mommy do for me when I'm upset and you *lend me your calm*?"

"Exactly!" he exclaimed.

"Maybe one day, I'll do *a comforting friend practice* for myself too," said Isabella. And with a tiny smile on her face, Isabella added,

"Right now, you and Mommy are my comforting friends and are teaching me how to grow one inside me.**"**

"Exactly," said her Papa.

Chapter 11

Carpentry Lessons

S ome days the *noticing stuff way of breathing* and *the elevator riding* Isabella would practice with her parents was boring. There were days Isabella didn't want to do them, and so she didn't, but most days she did. But,

> **"**Isabella always said the *good wishes practice* with her Mommy every night.**"**

Isabella said them for Pookie and for other living beings that she thought of. Once it was for all the fish in the ocean. Another time it was for an old elephant she had seen in the zoo. A few times she even said them for the kids at school, who used to be her friends, and now wouldn't play with her anymore.

One day, after Isabella and her Mommy had come back from the grocery store, everyone, including Pookie, was sitting comfortably on the living room couch.

"Okay Isabella," said Mommy, "it's time for you to learn how to hammer."

With an *amazed looking face*, Isabella sat up straight on the couch and in pretty loud voice asked, "Learn how to hammer what?"

"Nails of course," said her Mommy. "Don't you remember we said carpentry lessons would be part of the tumble taming plan?"

"I kind of remember," Isabella answered, "but I don't know what *carpentry* means."

"I'll explain it to you," said her Mommy. "Carpenters are people who build things. They build houses and sometimes they make beautiful wood furniture. They use hammers, nails and wood to do that. And, they use *carpentry skills* they were often taught at school."

While Mommy was talking, Papa got up from the couch, went into the kitchen and returned with a large purple basket. He handed the basket to Isabella. She looked inside and saw a shiny metal can filled with nails, a pair of goggles, a rainbow coloured hammer and a few clothespins.

Isabella picked up the hammer and noticed it wasn't too heavy or too big; it fit her hand perfectly. She wasn't sure what the clothespins or goggles were for. As Isabella was looking at all the items in the basket, her Mommy went to the closet by the backdoor of the apartment and took out a long, flat piece of wood and a green and blue striped yoga mat. Isabella watched as she doubled up the yoga mat, put it on the floor and placed the long wooden board on top of it.

"Come over here Isabella," said her Mommy, "and bring the basket along with you."

"Okay," said Isabella.

She walked over to where Mommy was sitting on the floor and plopped right down beside her.

"What's the yoga mat for?" Isabella asked.

"To stop the wooden board from moving around on the floor when you're hammering nails into it," her Mommy answered.

Isabella picked up the board and inspected it. It was heavy. It also smelled like the sap she would get on her hands when she picked up pinecones at the park near her apartment building.

"So, let's get this carpentry lesson started Isabella. Hand me a nail and pick up one for yourself too," said Mommy.

Isabella picked up a nail. She looked at it carefully. She touched one end and noticed it was sharp. She looked at the other end and noticed it had a flat top.

"Why is one end flat Mommy?" asked Isabella.

"It's a *roofer* nail. It has a bigger surface on top. That'll make it easier to hit."

"Anything else I need to know Mommy?"

"Well, just like we have names for the different parts of our bodies Isabella, so do nails. The part of the nail that you hit with the hammer is called *the head*. The long part of the nail is called *the shaft*. The sharp part that gets hammered into the wood is called *the point*."

"Does a hammer have names for all its parts too?" asked Isabella.

"Yes it does. We hit *the head* of the nail with the part of the hammer called *the face*. And, the rainbow coloured part of your hammer is called *the handle*."

Isabella shook her head from side to side and rolled her eyes, "Mommy, I know it's called a handle. What I don't know is what the goggles and clothespins are for?"

"Safety goggles will protect your eyes. Sometimes metal can fly off a nail when you hit it. Clothespins are to protect your fingers. Instead of holding the nail in place with your fingers you hold it in place with the clothespin. That way you won't hit your fingers if you miss hitting *the head* of the nail."

Isabella watched as Mrs. Pookapoo opened the clothespin and closed it on the nail's *shaft*. She placed *the point* of the nail on the part of the board she wanted to hammer the nail into.

"Now what do you think I do next Isabella?" asked Mommy.

"You'll hit *the head* of the nail with *the face* of the hammer!"

And that's exactly what her Mommy did. Bang – Bang – Bang, and she stopped. The nail was only half way into the board.

"Why aren't you hammering it all the way into the board?" asked Isabella.

"Because it will make it easier for you to pull the nails out when it's time," answered her Mommy.

"Time for what?" asked Isabella.

"For the last part of the tumble taming plan," said Mommy.

Mrs. Pookapoo looked at her daughter and started smiling.

"You look like you have a *question mark* on your face Isabella."

And of course, Isabella did. She actually had two questions.

Her Papa, who had been sitting near by listening and watching the carpentry lesson, answered both her questions.

"When am I supposed to hammer a nail into the board?" was her first question.

"Well, whenever your mad grows into a raging forest fire feeling inside you and a tumble flies out of your mouth; one of us will be right there with *you to lend you our calm.*"

When you feel you have enough *calm* of your own, that's when you hammer a nail half way into the board," was Papa's answer.

"Why do I have to hammer the nails in and later pull them out? It sounds kind of stupid to me."

"When I was practicing ways to have less tumbles I thought it sounded stupid too and I was wrong. It was a very important part of the taming the tumbles plan."

"Why Papa?"

"Because it *showed me* what mean, hurtful and unkind words can do to the people I say them to," he answered.

When it was time for Isabella to practice what her Mommy had taught her; each of the nails she hammered half way in – stayed in, and most of them stood up straight and tall. Isabella felt proud of herself. She couldn't help but wonder about what it was that Papa had been shown, by hammering the nails in and by pulling them out.

Pookie who had been watching and listening to all of the talking and loud banging was wondering the same thing. They both would just have to wait and see!

Chapter 12

What a Hug Can Do

Day by day and week by week, the Pookapoo family continued to practice together. They did the noticing way of breathing practice and elevator riding. At night, Isabella and her Mommy continued to say the good wishes practice for as many living beings as they could. Pookie especially liked it when he heard Isabella and her mommy saying the good wishes practice for him. *"May Pookie be happy."*... *"May Pookie be healthy and strong."*... *"May Pookie be safe."* ... *"May Pookie be kind to himself and to others."* Hearing such words reminded Pookie just how much Isabella loved him. It gave him a warm feeling in his heart.

As for the tumbles, any time Isabella got mad and the mad turned into mean words tumbling out of her mouth one of her *calm* parents just sat with her and *lent her their calm*. When Isabella noticed the fire inside her was almost out, she'd give the parent who was with her, the touch signal, and off she'd go to hammer after that.

Early one evening, after Isabella and her Papa had taken Pookie for a long walk they decided to stay outside a bit longer. While they were sitting outside on their apartment balcony, Isabella told her Papa an amazing thing that had happened to her at school that day.

"Today, one of the kids in my class put a birthday invitation on everyone's desk except mine. Some of the kids started making faces at me and quietly saying "Meanie Poo ... Meanie Poo." I could feel the tumbles were on their way Papa. But then, guess what happened?"

"I can't guess," said Papa. "Please, please tell me. I can't stand waiting."

"Oh Papa, sometimes slow is the way to go fast," Isabella said. Her Mommy had said the very same words to her not so long ago.

"I love your sense of humour Isabella, but please tell me what happened?"

"Okay...Okay. I will. First I did the *noticing stuff way* of breathing...then an elevator ride down to my feet...then toe wiggles in my socks... and then, a fast ride up to the top floor of my building."

"So what happened after that?"

"NOT ONE TUMBLE PAPA," shouted Isabella. "That's what happened after that!"

"Good for you Isabella!" exclaimed Papa.

"But it sounds like you had a very hard thing happen to you at school today - being left out like that. I think it's time for me to tell something else I learned about tumbles. My tumbles didn't just get started because I felt mad. Sometimes Isabella, my tumbles got started because I felt sad first.

"It's almost like mad was a hat that covered up my sad. And because it did, I didn't even know sad was inside me."

He jumped up from the lawn chair he was sitting on, went in the apartment and came back with a note pad and a pencil.

"I'll draw a picture for you Isabella, to help show you what I mean by *mad was a hat that covered up my sad.*" And that's what he did.

As Isabella looked at the drawing her Papa had made, her eyes quickly filled up with tears. The tears turned into tiny crystal coloured droplets and trickled down her cheeks.

"You're right Papa, I felt sad... after that, mad showed up. I *really* wanted to say mean things to hurt her ...like she hurt me."

"But you didn't," Papa said. "I can also see you're still hurting Isabella.

"What do you need right now that might help?"

Isabella raised both her little arms up towards him and said, "I need a big hug." And that's what he gave her. And it wasn't an ordinary hug. It was a hug that lasted for *30 wags of a puppy dog's tail* and that's a long, long time!

As her Papa hugged her, Isabella could feel her sad, *slowly, slowly,* melting away.

Pookie, who had been watching and listening to everything through the screen door knew hugs were the best medicine for almost anything, especially for thunderstorms.

Chapter 13

An Important Lesson

The days passed one by one. Isabella hardly ever had to hammer a nail into the wooden board. One Saturday morning, Isabella and her parents went for a long bike ride together. Pookie stayed home. He didn't mind that much. It gave him some time to catch up on his sleep.

Pookie also knew that when they came home from their bike ride he would be going to the park with them for a picnic lunch. He had seen them making sandwiches and putting them into the cooler. The heavenly smell of egg salad sandwiches still lingered in the air. The smell was making him hungry. He sure hoped they'd get back soon. His tummy was making those rumbling sounds again. At last he heard the key in the lock. They were home and they all looked hot and thirsty

"Let's have something to drink before we go to the park," said Mrs. Pookapoo. While they were having their drinks and talking about tumble taming, Pookie overheard Isabella telling her parents something he was sure they would be happy to hear. This is what Isabella said to them, word for word.

"Most times when I notice stuff about my breathing or take an elevator ride there's a quiet feeling in my body and in my brain."

"When I don't like something or I don't want to do it, I can feel mad is on its way. It's kind of like my body has an elastic band tightening inside it."

"Then what do you do?" Papa asked.

"I do my *noticing stuff way* of breathing or elevator riding. The *good wishes practice* you taught me Mommy comes into my head too. I even put my hand on my cheek sometimes ... like you do to me when I'm upset."

"What happens when you do those things?" Mommy asked.

Before Isabella answered, she smiled. It was the biggest smile her parents had ever seen from her.

"Most times it helps me be the boss of mad," she shouted. And I really like being the boss of somebody. And...that somebody is ME!"

"Sounds like you've learned the same lesson as I did," said her Papa.

"The only person I can really ever be the boss of is myself!"

This lesson helped me to have way fewer tumbles and much less mad."

Chapter 14

Dark Clouds and Silver Linings

After the picnic at the park and all the Pookapoos had returned home, it was time for Isabella's next lesson in tumble taming.

"Remember the nails and the wooden board Isabella?" asked her Mommy.

How could Isabella not remember! Each nail stood for a mean, hurtful word that had tumbled out of her mouth when she couldn't have things just the way she wanted them to be.

Isabella glanced towards the wooden board by the backdoor. There it lay, looking like a stretched out porcupine, all its quills standing straight up ... ready to attack.

"Now what?" Isabella asked.

"Time for each nail you hammered in to be pulled out!" Mommy answered.

So Isabella pulled out all the nails. It took a long time. There were a lot of nails. When she was finished the job, her Papa looked at her with his *serious parent face.* "Isabella, what do you see when you look at the top of the wooden board?"

"I see a lot of holes."

"And," Papa said, "those holes will *always* be in the wood. Saying mean, hurtful, unkind words to a person can do the same thing a nail can do. Words like that can leave a hole too. It can't be seen, like we can see the holes in the wood right now; but the hole can be felt inside. It's called hurting a person's feelings. Such a hole can take a long time to heal over and disappear".

"When you hurt a person's feelings often enough, what usually happens is they most often don't want to spend time with you or be your friend anymore."

"That's what happened to me Papa," Isabella said. "Nobody to play with me and no more friends. I cried at night in my bed. I felt sad and lonely inside."

"You found out what it felt like to be alone with nobody to play with. You had a tough situation Isabella that needed to be figured out - a problem."

"What's so important about all of this Isabella," said her Mommy, "is you were willing to let us help you, to listen and do the tumble taming practices. And I think we've all had lots of fun and got closer because of it.

"Sometimes something good can come out of something bad."

"That's what people call a dark cloud having a silver lining story," said Papa.

Isabella had heard her parents talk about dark clouds and silver linings before. She had never understood what it meant. Now she did...kind of.

After she got ready for bed that night, she decided to practice some belly button breathing with Snowy of course. Next, she did Mommy's *good wishes practices* for herself, Pookie, her Mommy and Papa and all the kids at school who no longer wanted to be her friends.   After she had finished doing that, she gave Pookie a *30 wags of a puppy dog's tail* hug. She knew for sure it was the right number of tail wags. She had counted how many times he wagged his short, white stubby tail while she was hugging him. Isabella slept well that night.

Pookie slept well too. Knowing his friend Isabella was feeling better inside made him feel *even happier than a snack could*. And in case you don't know anything about dogs, that's a very difficult thing for a dog to admit to - even one as kind and caring as Pookie.

The next morning, as Isabella was getting dressed, her parents could hear her humming what sounded like a happy tune. A few minutes later she arrived at the breakfast table and sat down with a thump. As she ate her oatmeal cereal and chewed on her banana, she told her Mommy and Papa something she had been thinking about since last night.

And this is what she said, word for word, "When I grow up I might become a carpenter and make beautiful wood furniture. That way, any nails that I hammer into the wood will stay in the wood, instead of leaving holes."

Isabella paused for a moment. Her brown eyes opened wide and a big grin lit up her face, "Growing up might take awhile," she said "and becoming a carpenter ...will have to wait. Some of the kids at school missed playing with me and want to give me another chance. They're all outside waiting for me to come down. They want me to go to the park with them and play tag."

"And, don't worry, I don't care if I do get tagged *it* now.

"Always being the best and having to be the boss of everything and everybody isn't any fun. It's lonely.**"**

"Wow," said her Mommy.

"Double wow," said her Papa.

"Thanks for all your help. And I'm sorry you had the tumbles Papa but I'm also kind of glad you did. That way, you were really able to teach me how to have less tumbles and get some friends back."

Pookie started to bark and run around in circles. He was so happy Isabella had friends again. And, he was glad she didn't cry anymore at night too. He was getting more sleep.

Just before she left the apartment to go out to play with her friends, Isabella Esmeralda Anastasia Pookapoo bent down close to Pookie and gave him a big hug. Then she kissed him right on his little black nose. She wanted to make sure Pookie knew, that no matter what might happen or how many friends she had; he would always be her *very* best friend!

And that is the end of the story about *How to Tame the Tumbles the Mindful Self-Compassionate Way.*

About the Author

Eileen Beltzner SCC BA MSW RSW

Special Care Counsellor, Registered Social Worker, Child & Family Therapist, Psychotherapist, & Certified Mindful Self-Compassion Teacher

Forty years ago my initial training was as a Special Care Counsellor in the parent-infant field. The published research project I was one of the authors of: *Reducing Stress in First-Time Mothers,* led to me writing a book called *The Handbook for First-Time Parents* and later a booklet, *Ups and Downs: A New Mother's Guide,* helping families distinguish between what was a Postpartum Mood Disorder (PPD) and what was not. I was very honored to receive the Mary Neville Award for my work. It is presented to people for their outstanding contributions towards prevention and early intervention in children's mental health services. Receiving this award validated my efforts, my passion and my drive to continue to work for the next 15 years towards reducing the stigma, silence and ignorance surrounding PPD and developing support services for postpartum families. This work cumulated in the creation of a national

Canadian organization, Postpartum Adjustment Support Services – Canada (PASS-CAN). Reaching out and connecting with other countries worldwide, eventually led to my becoming the President of Postpartum Support International (PSI).

Since that time I have had many rich experiences and adventures as a life long student learning my craft, as a Child and Family Therapist, as a wife, a mother, a daughter, a sister and a happy and sometimes struggling human being.

My MSC adventure began, when along with my husband Rainer, we experienced the benefits of the MSC training program because we were struggling in our personal life. MSC really helped us and we wanted to pass it on to others in Canada; so...we both became Certified MSC Teachers. We are both on the Faculty of the Centre for Mindfulness Studies in Toronto, Canada where we teach the 8-week MSC version and the 5-day MSC intensive, to all sorts of wonderful people.

And now I've become a Nana to a delightful little human being whose name is Samuel. His entry into the world, a few short years ago, has returned me to my first passion – supporting parents in "raising up" all the children depending on them for their happiness...health... strength...safety...and kindness. My wish is that this story, *How to Tame the Tumbles the Mindful Self-Compassionate Way* will contribute to supporting parents in doing just that!

Notes & Resources

Time - in and Time - out

When I recommended the book *Time-in Parenting,* (2002), by the late Otto Weininger Ph.D. to parents with children who were having behavioral challenges, time-in wasn't what most daycares, schools, pediatricians or child experts were recommending at the time. Using time-out was often their answer. "*Time-in Parenting,* is a guide for parents to help their children develop emotional self-control, life skills, and problem solving by staying connected with their attachment figure. Time-in gives an upset child what she needs most...her parents."

The Whole-Brain Child: 12 Revolutionary Strategies to Nurture Your Child's Developing Mind by Daniel Siegel, MD and Tina Payne Bryson, Ph.D. (2012), is a short, readable and practical book that explains in layman's terms why it's so important *not* to isolate the child when he or she is emotionally distraught. "Decades of research in attachment demonstrate that particularly in times of distress, we need to be near and be soothed by the people who care for us. But when children lose emotional control, parents often put them in their room or by themselves in the *naughty chair*, meaning that in this moment of emotional distress they have to suffer alone."

A review of *The Whole-Brain Child* written by Diana Divecha, Ph.D., a developmental psychologist and research affiliate of the Yale Center for Emotional Intelligence, is available online (greatergood.berkeley.edu).

Time-ins for Parents

Most parents often have busy, hectic and stressed out lives. If time-in is needed for anything, it is to give your brain a rest by resetting it. How? By practicing some intentional mindfulness pauses through out your day. I like to call them mini time-ins. It will help give you that extra calm definitely needed, *to lend your calm* to a child having a full-blown tumble.

Mini time-ins offer your brain some uninterrupted time in the present moment, during what can often be an action packed day of giving out. A mini time-in can be easily incorporated into your day; and will not add more items to your *to do list*.

For example; all of us need to eat or drink something every so often; so that's where you can introduce a mindfulness practice pause into your day. How? Choose a mealtime and then before you begin just start by noticing what the food you are eating or drinking looks like. For instance, what colors are present? What smells do you notice? Once you begin, noticing the taste and perhaps the texture or temperature of your food or beverage. While you are chewing or swallowing for instance, can you hear any sounds? Continue paying attention to whatever else captures your attention about your food. Each time you notice your mind has stopped paying attention to what you are eating or drinking and you are deep in thought about the past or the future, ...just return to paying attention to your food, bringing yourself back into the present moment. It's as simple as that. Once finished your meal, congratulate yourself on your efforts. You have just strengthened *your paying attention on purpose part of your brain* and practiced a few moments of mindfulness.

Another example of a mini time-in is choosing, from time to time, to pay attention in a particular way to walking. Each time you take a step, perhaps when you go for a bathroom break, walk from meeting to meeting or go for a short walk outdoors you can practice mindful walking. How? With each step you take, focus your attention on the sole of your foot each time one of your feet touches the ground. Each time you notice your mind is somewhere else, and your not paying attention to the soles of your feet, return to paying attention to the feeling the pressure in the soles of your feet each time they make contact with the surface you are walking on. Practicing mindful walking regularly can be a powerful mini time-in. This practice will allow you to bring your mind into the present moment and give you a short break from the constant, often negative chatter in your head. You don't have to believe me of course, just try it for a few weeks and see if it's right for you.

For parents wanting information about and practice links to Mindful Self-Compassion Time-ins, read Maryam Abdulla's essay "Self-Compassion for Parents" online.

More information about mindful walking, a formal walking practice (available at Jackkornfield.com) and Dr. Shawna Shapiro's TED Talk (available on YouTube) has more information about the power of mindfulness.

Watch Dr. Matt Killingsworth's TED talk " Want to be Happier? Stay in the Moment" (available on YouTube) for more information about why mini time-ins can help you to be happier.

What a Hug Can Do

When we hug a person or a pet we are connecting with them through touch. Every hug in *How to Tame the Tumbles the Mindful Self-Compassionate Way* lasts for 30 wags of a puppy dog's tail; that's just about 20 seconds. Studies have shown a twenty second hug reduces the harmful, physical effects of stress, including its impact on blood pressure and heart rate. This happens because hugging releases oxytocin, a powerful hormone that acts like a neurotransmitter in the brain.

Dacher Keltner, Ph.D., the founding director of the Greater Good Science Center and a professor of psychology at the University of California, Berkeley, explains other reasons why touch is so important in his paper "Hands On Research: The Science of Touch" (available online).

Mommy's Good Wishes Practice

My Mommy's Good Wishes Practice is what is known as a Loving Kindness Meditation (LKM). Emma Seppälä, Ph.D. (emmaseppala.com), the Science Director of Stanford University's Center for Compassion and Altruism Research list 18 science-based reasons why my *Mommy's Good Wishes Practice* is not only good for children but for grown-ups too.

Greater Happiness in 5 Minutes a Day, written by Christine Carter, Ph.D., will give you suggestions on how to teach a Loving Kindness Meditation (LKM) to a child.

My full length audio of *Mommy's Good Wishes Practice,* and other practices found in this book, are available online (mindfulselfcompassiontraining.podbean.com).

The Noticing Stuff Way of Breathing

Just Breathe by Julie Bayer Saltzman and Josh Saltzman is a short film (available on YouTube) that demonstrates how *the noticing stuff way of breathing*–Isabella's parents introduced her to, *can* help both child and adult feel more calm inside when mad starts to show up.

Children and Mindfulness

When I was practicing as a Child and Family Therapist, part of my job was to recommend books to parents so they might learn more about the course of action I was recommending as part of a treatment plan for their child. To do this I had to keep abreast of works by leading professional in that particular field. My recommendation to any parent or professional reading this book wanting to source gold standard books and information in the field of mindfulness, children and teens is to check out Dr. Amy Saltzman (www.stillquietplace.com). Dr. Saltzman or Dr. Amy, as children and youth sometimes call her, is recognized by her peers as a visionary and pioneer in the fields of holistic medicine and mindfulness for kids, teens, parents, teachers, therapists, and allied professionals.

Mindful Self-Compassion (MSC) Connections

The Centre for Mindful-Self Compassion website (www. centerformsc.org) is the official site to go to for information about Mindful Self-Compassion training for both adults and teens in your part of the world; and, also to find many informative YouTube talks, resources and audios of guided Mindful Self-Compassion practices.

Kristin Neff's website (www.selfcompassion.org) has many resources including compilations of research studies, YouTube talks, self-compassion quiz, etc.

Christopher Germer's website (www.mindfulselfcompassion. org) has publications and audio of guided meditations.

Eileen and Rainer Beltzner's website (www. selfcompassionsolutions.com) has links to resources, audios, and upcoming training and events.

Kristy Arbon's HeartWorks Training (www.kristyarbon. com) is an organization dedicated to training, mentoring, and ongoing support in self-compassion and mindfulness practices online, in person and internationally.

The Centre for Mindfulness Studies (www. mindfulnessstudies.com) is a charity located in Toronto, Canada and is a distinguished leader in the professional training, research and delivery of mindfulness-based interventions. The Centre offers evidence-based training programs: mindfulness-based cognitive therapy (MBCT), mindfulness-based stress reduction (MBSR) and Mindful

Self-Compassion Training (MSC). Eileen Beltzner is a Faculty member at the Centre as is her husband Rainer Beltzner. They teach the 8-week and 5-day Intensive Mindful Self-Compassion training course here several times a year.

Mindful Self-Compassion Books

Germer, C. K. & Neff, K. D. *The Mindful Self-Compassion Workbook: A Proven Way to Accept Yourself, Build Inner Strength, and Thrive.* New York: Guilford Press (2018).

Bluth, K. *The Self-Compassion Workbook for Teens: Mindfulness and Compassion Skills to Overcome Self-Criticism and Embrace Who You Are.* Oakland: New Harbinger Publications, Inc. (2017).

Neff, K. *Self-Compassion: The Proven Power of Being Kind to Yourself.* New York: William Morrow and Company (2011). (Also available as an audiobook)

Germer, C. K. *The Mindful Path to Self-Compassion: Freeing Yourself from Destructive Thoughts and Emotions.* New York: Guilford Press (2009). (Also available as an audio book)

Mindful Self-Compassion & Mindfulness Books for Professionals

Germer, C. K., & Neff, K. D. *Teaching the Mindful Self-Compassion Program: A Guide for Professionals.* New York: Guilford Press (2019).

Germer, C. K., Siegel, R. D. & Fulton, P. R. *Mindfulness and Psychotherapy*. New York: Guilford Press (2016).

Germer, C. K. & Siegel, R. D. *Wisdom and Compassion in Psychotherapy*. New York: Guilford Press (2014).

Treleaven, D. A. *Trauma-Sensitive Mindfulness. (Practices for Safe and Transformative Healing)*. New York: W.W. Norton & Company, Inc. (2018).

Kabat – Zinn, J. *"Full Catastrophe Living: Using the Wisdom of Your Body and Mind to Face Stress, Pain and Illness (Revised Edition)."* New York: Bantam Books (2013).

Other Websites

Kelty Mental Health Resource Centre (keltymentalhealth. ca) is an outstanding resource. It has a mindfulness section second to none. Free guided meditation audio recordings, links to mindfulness resources, and a video of youth sharing their experience with mindfulness.

Mindfulness Everyday (www.mindfulnesseveryday.org), a registered charitable organization in Toronto, Canada has assembled a dedicated team of professionals, experienced in conducting mindfulness workshops, in non-clinical settings, as well as programs for youth, parents and educators and book recommendations and resources for parents and their children.

Mindful Schools (www.mindfulschools.org), is one of the key players in the movement to integrate mindfulness into the everyday learning environment of K-12 classrooms. The organization has trained over 25,000 educators, parents, and mental health professionals who work with youth.

Films by Mindful Schools

Healthy Habits of Mind (2017) is a 41-minute documentary created by filmmaker Mette Bahnsen exploring how neuroscience explains the value of mindfulness in education.

Room to Breathe (2013) is a 56-minute documentary "exploring the personal transformations that happen for students, their families, and educators as mindfulness is introduced in a truly challenging public school environment. By providing a raw and realistic look at the experience, it shows how integrating mindfulness, along with patience, skill, collaboration and more, can transform even the most difficult classrooms."

Online Resources for Teachers

"Mindfulness: A Guide for Teachers" (PDF), by Dr. Amy Saltzman
"How Self-Compassion can Help Teachers Prevent Teacher Burnout" by Vicki Zakrzewski, Ph.D., Education Director of the Greater Good Science Center

Acknowledgements

I wish to thank a number of people in my life for their unique contributions to this book. Many of you shared your wisdom, your time, and your life experiences, both personal and professional. Many of you offered your encouragement, your love, your compassion, your patience and your deep belief that this book was an important book that had to be written. And many of you contributed to keeping me well and healthy in body, mind and spirit. And one *little* person just made me laugh! This book would never have become a reality without each and everyone of you.

My dear husband Rainer Beltzner, Mary Walker, Nolan Machan, my son Stephen Beltzner, my daughter Carrie Anne Beltzner, my grandson Samuel Brunet, my late sister Kristine Dufour, my sister Kareen and my brother-in-law John Jackson, my sister-in law Judy Beltzner and my brother-in-law Klaus Beltzner, my Great Niece Ella and Great Nephew Rowan Jackson-Cappuccino, my Great Nephews Quinlan and Maxwell Jackson-Kelly, my Great Niece Cassie Brunet and her mother Jan Soutermans, the late Paul Donovan, Dr. Pamela Stewart, Barbara Mongrain, Dirk Gebhardt, Dr. Patricia Rockman, Dr. Evan Collins, David Dennis ND, Francesco Paglialunga, Zindel

Segal Ph.D., Melvina Walter, Amy Land, Ashley Flis Ph.D., Patricia Ward, Cheryl Blackington, Dr. Nishanthie Dolage, Jan Vinnai, Dr. Alison Arnot, Ermina Tsounis, Dr. Alison Kelford, Nancy Fornasiero, Annette Boden, Tina Gibson, and my publisher Howard Aster.

To My Mindfulness and Mindful Self-Compassion Colleagues:

Dr. Amy Saltzman, I am deeply appreciative of all the time you spent reading and re-reading multiple drafts of *How to Tame the Tumbles the Mindful Self-Compassionate Way*. You could have easily said no when I asked you to give me your thoughts good and bad, about my manuscript. We had only met briefly at a talk you were giving in Toronto, Canada. You didn't even hesitate to help out, though you said you would be tough because that was what helped you to write your best. You provided wonderful constructive criticism, thoughtful comments and suggestions. You were also very kind about it. Thank you from the bottom of my heart. Your contributions to this book were invaluable. I hope "I've finally got it right!"

Christopher Germer, Ph.D. Thank you for all your clinical wisdom in developing a MSC training program that helps people learn how to give themselves compassion when suffering arises – not to get rid of it but because they are suffering. Thank you for sharing your excitement about *How to Tame the Tumbles the Mindful Self-Compassionate Way* and *making it easy for me*. Thanks for being who you are and for being busy making a difference in the world.

Kristin Neff, Ph.D. Thank you for your empirically based, groundbreaking research that continues to demonstrate the correlation between higher levels of self-compassion and well being. Thank you for your generosity in sharing yourself and your research with others. Thank you for developing a course that teaches self-compassion *explicitly*. And thank-you for telling me it is a very *sweet* book.

Steven Hickman, Psy.D. I was very happy to get all your enthusiastic comments and thoughtful suggestions to make this book the best it could be. And of course, thank you for your support, direction and mentorship in my first and final steps in completing the requirements necessary to become a Certified Mindful Self-Compassion Teacher. Your kindness, knowledge, encouragement, expertise and humour were very much appreciated. It was great to learn from one of the best.

Manufactured by Amazon.ca
Bolton, ON

25745161R00048